Look

STARTER

A Reading Anthology for Young Learners

LUCY CRICHTON

NATIONAL GEOGRAPHIC
LEARNING

Australia • Brazil • Canada • Mexico • Singapore • United Kingdom • United States

Contents

Drive Along, Animal Song

Drive, drive, drive along.
Come on now,
Let's sing a song!

Off we go,
You and me.
Sing along,
Lots to see!

What's your name?

Say hello.

Come on, horse,

Time to go!

Sing, sing, sing along.

Come on, rabbit,

Here's a song!

How are you?
I'm fine, thank you.
Come on, cow,
Lots to do!

Sing, sing, sing along.

Come on, cat,

Here's a song!

Sit down
And say hello.
Stand up, dog,
And off we go!

Toys in the Snow

White, white, it's all white!

What's this?

13

14

It's Lunchtime

16

17

18

19

The Empty Pot

I want to find a new emperor.

This is the emperor of China. He's old.

Ping's mom, dad, and brother help him.

I have soil.

I have water.

I have a pot.

I'm sad. I want a flower.

The children have flowers for the emperor,

but the emperor isn't happy.

Ping is sad.

Muddy Puddles!

It's Forest School today. Come on! Let's play!

Look! Rain!
Pitter, patter, pitter, patter.

How many puddles?
Lots of puddles!

30

I can splash! Splash, splash, splash!

I can kick the water!

I can jump!

What a great day!

Little Red Hen

I can make bread!

Little Red Hen is busy.

36

37

38

Activities

STORY 1 Drive Along, Animal Song

Look and match.

2 Toys in the Snow

Look and color. Circle.

1.

It's a ball. It's **brown** / **yellow.**

2.

It's a train. It's **white** / **red**.

3.

It's a car. It's **orange** / **black**.

4.

It's a doll. It's **blue** / **green**.

5.

It's a robot. It's **yellow** / **blue**.

STORY 3 It's Lunchtime

Read and draw or . Match.

1. I don't like milk.

A.

2. I don't like rice.

B.

3. I like chicken dinosaurs.

C.

4. I like juice.

D.

5. I don't like water.

E.

6. I like bread.

F.

STORY 4 # The Empty Pot

Find and circle. Match.

This is my family.

1.

mom

2.

dad

3.

brother

d	x	c	m	m	l	p	b	l	k
d	a	d	p	o	m	q	r	j	w
v	w	e	y	m	n	t	o	u	t
d	r	s	t	u	o	s	t	y	p
s	i	s	t	e	r	b	h	o	s
e	f	d	h	o	p	q	e	d	n
g	r	a	n	d	m	a	r	u	k
d	h	e	g	r	a	n	d	p	a

4.

sister

5.

grandma

6.

grandpa

Muddy Puddles!

Count and circle.

How many puddles?

1.  six / (seven)

2. 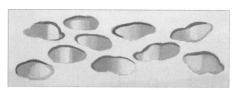 ten / eleven

3.  thirteen / fourteen

4.  nine / nineteen

5.  seven / eight

6.  twelve / twenty

Little Red Hen

Look and circle.

1. I (can) / can't help.

2. I can / can't help.

3. I can / can't help.

4. I can / can't help.

5. I can / can't help.

6. I can / can't help.

NATIONAL GEOGRAPHIC LEARNING

National Geographic Learning,
a Cengage Company

*Look Starter: A Reading Anthology for
Young Learners*
Lucy Crichton

Publisher: Sherrise Roehr

Executive Editor: Eugenia Corbo

Publishing Consultant: Karen Spiller

Senior Development Editor: Mary Whittemore

Associate Development Editor: Jen Williams-Rapa

Director of Global Marketing: Ian Martin

Heads of Strategic Marketing:

    Charlotte Ellis (Europe, Middle East
    and Africa)

    Kiel Hamm (Asia)

    Irina Pereyra (Latin America)

Product Marketing Manager: David Spain

Senior Director of Production: Michael Burggren

Senior Content Project Manager: Nick Ventullo

Media Researchers: Leila Hishmeh, Jeff Millies

Art Director: Brenda Carmichael

Manufacturing Planner: Mary Beth Hennebury

Composition: SPi Global

For permission to use material from this text or product,
submit all requests online at **cengage.com/permissions**
Further permissions questions can be emailed to
permissionrequest@cengage.com

ISBN: 978-0-357-02757-8

National Geographic Learning
5191 Natorp Boulevard
Mason, OH 45040
USA

Locate your local office at **international.cengage.com/region**

Visit National Geographic Learning online at **ELTNGL.com**
Visit our corporate website at **www.cengage.com**

Credits

Cover: © Joel Sartore/National Geographic Creative.

Photos: 3 © ESB Professional/Shutterstock.com; **4** © Sara Code-Kroll/Shutterstock Offset; **5** © Tomsickova Tatyana/Shutterstock.com; **6** © alexkatkov/Shutterstock.com; **7** © FatCamera/E+/Getty Images; **8** © Adrian Vaju Photography/Shutterstock.com; **27** © Imgorthand/E+/Getty Images; **28** © SolStock/E+/Getty Images; **29** © Yuganov Konstantin/Shutterstock.com; **30** © Ben Welsh/SuperStock; **31** © Westend61/Getty Images. **32** © Ambre Haller/Moment/Getty Images; **33** © Aleksandra Suzi/Shutterstock.com; **34** © oliveromg/Shutterstock.com.

Illustrations: 9–14, 43 Patrick Corrigan/Astound Art; **15–20, 44** Vipin Jacob/Lemonade Agency; **21–26, 45** Giuliano Aloisi/Advocate Art; **35–41, 47** Julie Colombet/Astound Art; **42** Elisa Chavarri/Painted Words; **46** Felia Hanakata/Lemonade Agency.

Printed in the United States of America
Print Number: 08   Print Year: 2024

Look Teacher's Resources and Audio
ELTNGL.com/look